CFP® Certification Exam Flashcard Review Book

Investment Planning

Written by
Matthew Brandeburg, CFP®

A publication of
Coventry House Publishing

CONTENTS

CFP® Certification Exam Flashcard Review Book: Investment Planning

INVESTMENT PLANNING

LIQUIDITY & MARKETABILITY

MONEY MARKET FUNDS

LIQUIDITY & MARKETABILITY

- Liquidity is the ability to buy or sell an investment quickly and at a known price without incurring a significant loss of value
- Marketability is the speed and ease with which a security may be bought or sold

---

MONEY MARKET FUNDS

- Invest in low-risk, short-term investments such as CDs, commercial paper, and Treasury bills
- The underlying investments within money market funds have an average maturity of 30 to 90 days
- Easily converted to cash
- Low default risk
- Low real return

CERTIFICATE OF DEPOSIT (CD)

COMMERCIAL PAPER

CERTIFICATE OF DEPOSIT (CD)

- Deposit made with a financial institution for a specific period of time
- The financial institution pays the investor a fixed rate of interest for the term of the certificate. At the end of the term, the investor redeems the CD and receives the original amount of money deposited.
- CDs may lose value if not held to maturity
- Negotiable CDs are short-term, fixed-income securities that may be bought or sold in the open market at a market-determined price

---

COMMERCIAL PAPER

- Unsecured promissory note issued by a corporation
- Issued in denominations of $100,000 or more
- Has a maturity of 270 days or less
- Higher default risk than Treasury bills

EURODOLLARS

BOND

EURODOLLARS

- US dollar denominated deposits located in banks outside the US
- Subject to less regulation than similar deposits located in banks within the US
- Not subject to oversight by the Federal Reserve
- Eurodollars do not involve only deposits held in European banks

---

BOND

- An agreement in which a bondholder loans money to a bond issuer for a specific period of time at a predetermined rate of interest
- Bondholder receives semiannual fixed interest payments throughout the life of the bond
- Interest payments are determined by the bond's credit quality and duration
- At maturity, the bondholder receives the face value of the bond
- Bonds may lose value if not held to maturity

BOND ISSUERS

BOND RATINGS

BOND ISSUERS

- Federal, state, and local governments
- Agencies of the government
- Corporations

BOND RATINGS

- Investment grade bond
  - Rated BBB- or higher by Standard & Poor's
  - Rated Baa3 or higher by Moody's
- High yield bond
  - Rated of BB+ or lower by Standard & Poor's
  - Rated Ba1 or lower by Moody's

COUPON RATE

YIELD TO MATURITY (YTM)

COUPON RATE

- The stated annual interest rate that is paid to a bondholder each period for the term of a bond
- Typically paid semiannually to maturity
- Example: A $1,000 bond with a 5% coupon will pay a bondholder $50 per year

---

YIELD TO MATURITY (YTM)

- YTM is a bond's rate of return if interest payments are reinvested at an equal rate and the bond is held to maturity
- Higher risk bonds have higher yields to maturity
- If a bond's coupon rate is greater than its YTM, the bond will sell at a premium
- If a bond's coupon rate is equal to its YTM, the bond will sell at par value
- If a bond's coupon rate is less than its YTM, the bond will sell at a discount

BOND PREMIUMS & DISCOUNTS

BOND RELATIONSHIPS

BOND PREMIUMS & DISCOUNTS

- If a bond is selling at a premium to par, the YTM will be less than the coupon rate
- If a bond is selling at par, the YTM will be equal to the coupon rate
- If a bond is selling at a discount to par, the YTM will be greater than the coupon rate

_____

BOND RELATIONSHIPS

- The lower a bond's coupon rate, the lower the reinvestment risk
- The lower a bond's coupon rate, the greater the relative price fluctuation
- The longer a bond's term to maturity, the greater the relative price fluctuation
- Higher inflation leads to higher interest rates, which leads to lower bond values

DURATION

DURATION RELATIONSHIPS

DURATION

- A measure of the length of time it takes for the price of a bond to be repaid through its internal cash flows
- Duration is affected by a bond's coupon rate, time to maturity, and interest rate
- By matching a portfolio's bond duration to the investment time horizon, an investor can reduce interest rate risk and immunize his or her portfolio
- Duration of a zero-coupon bond is equal to the bond's term to maturity
- Duration of a coupon bond is less than the bond's term to maturity

———————————

DURATION RELATIONSHIPS

- The lower a bond's coupon rate, the greater the bond's duration
- The longer a bond's term to maturity, the greater the bond's duration
- The lower a bond's duration, the lower the interest rate risk

BOND HEDGING STRATEGIES

CALLABLE BOND

BOND HEDGING STRATEGIES

- <u>Bond barbell</u>: Investment strategy in which both short-term and long-term bonds are purchased
- <u>Bond bullet</u>: Investment strategy in which several non-callable bonds are purchased that mature at the same time
- <u>Bond ladder</u>: Investment strategy in which an equal amount of money is invested into a series of bonds with staggered maturity dates

---

CALLABLE BOND

- A bond that may be redeemed by the issuer during a specific time period at a predetermined price
- Protects the bond issuer from a decline in interest rates
- Callable bonds offer higher coupon rates than non-callable bonds issued for the same term by the same issuer

SINKING-FUND PROVISION

REGISTERED BONDS &
BEARER BONDS

SINKING-FUND PROVISION

- Provision in a bond agreement that allows the issuer to retire a portion of the debt each year, or at predetermined intervals
- Reduces a bond issuer's interest rate risk because as market interest rates decline the issuer will replace a portion of the existing debt with lower yielding bonds
- Bonds with a sinking fund provision offer higher coupon rates than bonds without a sinking fund provision issued for the same term by the same issuer

---

REGISTERED BONDS & BEARER BONDS

- Registered bond
  - A bond whose owner is registered with the organization or entity that issued the debt
  - Coupon payments are made to the owner of record
  - Registered bonds are more secure than bearer bonds
- Bearer bond
  - Coupon payments are made to the person who physically holds the bond
  - Actual coupons may be attached to the bond. It's the bondholder's responsibility to submit coupons to the issuer for payment.
  - Bearer bonds can be transferred like cash

ZERO-COUPON BOND

_____

I BOND

ZERO-COUPON BOND

- A bond that is sold at a deep discount from face value
- Does not pay interest prior to maturity
- Taxes must be paid on accrued interest each year even though no interest is received by the bondholder
- Taxable zero-coupon bonds are best positioned in tax-deferred accounts
- Zero-coupon bonds have no reinvestment risk
- Duration of a zero-coupon bond is equal to the bond's term to maturity

---

I BOND

- Inflation-protected savings bond issued by the US Treasury Department
- I bond interest rates adjust semiannually to correspond with changes in inflation as measured by the Consumer Price Index (CPI)
- Guaranteed to never lose value, even during deflationary periods
- Final maturity is 30 years from the date of issue
- I bond interest is taxed at the federal level only

EE BOND

EE BOND
INTEREST EXCLUSION

EE BOND

- Education savings bond issued by the US Treasury Department
- Sold at a deep discount equal to half the bond's face value
- May be purchased for a minimum price of $25 (for a $50 bond) and a maximum price of $5,000 (for a $10,000 bond)
- At a minimum, the US Treasury Department guarantees the value of an EE bond will double after 20 years
- Final maturity is 30 years from the date of issue
- EE Bonds issued after May 1, 2005 earn a fixed interest rate

---

EE BOND
INTEREST EXCLUSION

- EE bond interest is excluded from a taxpayer's income if the following requirements are met:
  - Proceeds must be used to pay for qualified higher education expenses for the bond owner, his or her spouse, or dependent
  - Bond owner must be at least 24 years old when the bond is issued
  - Bond must have been issued after December 31, 1989
- The interest exclusion is phased out for high income taxpayers and is not available for married taxpayers filing a separate tax return

MUNICIPAL BOND

_____

TYPES OF MUNICIPAL BONDS

MUNICIPAL BOND

- A bond issued by a state, county, city, or other municipality
- Interest is not taxed at the federal level
- Interest is tax-exempt in most states if the bondholder lives in the state in which the bond is issued
- Municipal bonds are well-suited for individuals in high tax brackets

---

TYPES OF MUNICIPAL BONDS

- General obligation bond
- Revenue bond
- Private activity bond

GENERAL OBLIGATION BOND

REVENUE BOND

GENERAL OBLIGATION BOND

- Municipal bond issued by a state or local government to finance the general operations, programs, and functions of the issuing body
- Bondholders are repaid through tax revenue

REVENUE BOND

- Municipal bond issued by a state or local government to finance a specific project, such as an airport, power plant, prison, public transportation system, stadium, toll bridge, or toll road
- Bondholders are repaid through revenue generated from the project being financed

PRIVATE ACTIVITY BOND

CORPORATE BOND

PRIVATE ACTIVITY BOND

- Municipal bond issued by a state or local government to finance a private project that does not constitute the normal function of government
- Bondholders are repaid through revenue generated from the project being financed
- Interest earned on private activity bonds is an AMT preference item

---

CORPORATE BOND

- A bond that is issued by a public or private corporation
- Bondholders are repaid through income earned from corporate operations
- Physical assets owned by the corporation may be used as collateral
- Coupon rates are determined by the credit quality of the corporation. As credit quality increases, coupon rates will decrease.

CONVERTIBLE BOND

SECURED BOND

CONVERTIBLE BOND

- Corporate bond that may be converted into common stock of the issuing corporation
- May be converted at the bondholder's discretion
- Allows an investor to share in the growth of the corporation if the bond is converted into common stock
- Because of their flexibility, convertible bonds offer lower coupon rates than non-convertible bonds issued for the same term by the same issuer
- Conversion value = $[\text{Par} / \text{CP}] \times P_s$

SECURED BOND

- A bond that is secured by collateral
- Secured bondholders have a legal claim to specific assets if the issuer defaults or becomes insolvent
- An example of a secured bond is a mortgage bond backed by real estate

DEBENTURE BOND

INDENTURE AGREEMENT

DEBENTURE BOND

- A debenture bond is an unsecured bond issued by a government or private entity
- Debenture bonds are only backed by the general credit of the issuer
- Debenture bondholders have the same rights as general creditors
- Because of their higher default risk, debenture bonds offer higher coupon rates than secured bonds issued for the same term by the same issuer

----

INDENTURE AGREEMENT

- Formal contract between a bond issuer and a bondholder
- Describes the terms and conditions of a bond including:
    - Issue amount
    - Maturity date
    - How coupon payments are determined
    - When coupon payments are made
    - Description of collateral
    - Call provisions

PROMISSORY NOTE

_____

TREASURY INVESTMENT
TERMS TO MATURITY

PROMISSORY NOTE

- Unconditional promise to pay a sum of money to a payee on demand, or at a predetermined future date
- Terms of the note include the principal amount, interest rate, and maturity date
- Unsecured promissory notes are only backed by the general credit of the issuer
- Secured promissory notes are backed by collateral

———————————

TREASURY INVESTMENT TERMS TO MATURITY

- Treasury bills have maturities of 1 year or less
- Treasury notes have maturities of 10 years or less
- Treasury bonds have maturities of 30 years or less

TREASURY BILL

_____

TREASURY NOTE

TREASURY BILL

- Issued by the US Treasury Department
- Sold at a discount from face value in minimum denominations of $100
- Does not pay interest prior to maturity
- Has a maturity of one year or less
- Taxed at the federal level only

TREASURY NOTE

- Issued by the US Treasury Department
- Sold in minimum denominations of $100
- Fixed interest payments are made semiannually to maturity
- Has a maturity of ten years or less
- Taxed at the federal level only

TREASURY BOND

TREASURY STRIPS

TREASURY BOND

- Issued by the US Treasury Department
- Sold in minimum denominations of $100
- Fixed interest payments are made semiannually to maturity
- Has a maturity of thirty years or less
- Taxed at the federal level only

TREASURY STRIPS

- Separate Trading of Registered Interest and Principal Securities
- STRIPS include Treasury notes, Treasury bonds, and TIPS whose interest and principal portions have been separated so they may be sold individually on the secondary market
- Sold at a discount from face value
- Does not pay interest prior to maturity
- Taxes must be paid on accrued interest each year even though no interest is received by the investor

TREASURY INFLATION PROTECTED SECURITY (TIPS)

COMMON STOCK

TREASURY INFLATION PROTECTED SECURITY (TIPS)

- Financial security indexed to the rate of inflation as measured by the Consumer Price Index (CPI)
- TIPS pay interest every six months
- Interest payments increase with inflation and decrease with deflation
- Investors are paid either the adjusted principal amount at maturity, or the original principal amount, whichever is greater
- TIPS have maturities of 5, 10, or 30 years
- TIPS are taxed at the federal level only

COMMON STOCK

- Security that represents partial ownership in a corporation
- Common stock generates income and growth for investors through dividends and capital appreciation
- Provides a long-term hedge against inflation
- In the event of corporate bankruptcy, common stockholders receive funds after preferred stockholders, bondholders, and creditors

BLUE CHIP STOCK

GROWTH STOCK

BLUE CHIP STOCK

- Blue chip stocks are highly regarded, well-established companies that have demonstrated the ability to operate profitably in both positive and negative economic climates
- Blue chip stocks pay dividends and provide a long-term hedge against inflation
- The Dow Jones Industrial Average consists of 30 blue chip stocks

---

GROWTH STOCK

- A stock whose earnings are expected to grow at an above-average rate relative to the overall market
- Growth stocks do not pay large dividends because earnings are reinvested back into the company
- Growth stocks include:
    - High-tech companies
    - Pharmaceutical companies

CYCLICAL STOCK

DEFENSIVE STOCK

CYCLICAL STOCK

- A stock that increases in value during the expansion and peak stages of the business cycle, and decreases in value during the contraction and trough stages of the business cycle
- Cyclical stocks include:
  - Airlines
  - Automobiles
  - Construction companies
  - Manufacturing companies
  - Railroads
  - Steel companies

DEFENSIVE STOCK

- A stock that maintains a stable value during all stages of the business cycle
- Defensive stocks include:
  - Food companies
  - Healthcare companies
  - Non-durable goods
  - Oil companies
  - Tobacco companies
  - Utilities

INTEREST SENSITIVE STOCK

STOCK MARKET
BENCHMARKS & INDEXES

INTEREST SENSITIVE STOCK

- A stock whose value is sensitive to changes in interest rates
- Interest sensitive stocks include:
  - Banks
  - Brokerage houses
  - Insurance companies
  - Savings and loans
  - Utilities

STOCK MARKET
BENCHMARKS & INDEXES

- <u>Dow Jones Industrial Average</u>: Price-weighted average of 30 blue chip US stocks
- <u>EAFE Index</u>: Value weighted index of the equity performance of Europe, Australia, and the Far East
- <u>NASDAQ Composite</u>: Value weighted index of all the stocks traded on the NASDAQ market
- <u>Russell 2000</u>: Value weighted index measuring the performance of 2,000 small-cap US stocks
- <u>S&P 500</u>: Value weighted index of 500 widely-held US stocks
- <u>Wilshire 5000</u>: Value weighted index measuring the overall performance of the US stock market

WASH SALE

DIVIDEND DATES

WASH SALE

- A wash sale occurs if an investor acquires substantially identical stock during the 30 days prior to, or 30 days following the date of sale
- If a wash sale occurs, no loss deduction is allowed, and the amount of the disallowed loss must be added to the cost basis of the newly acquired shares
- Wash sale rules apply to the investor rather than to a particular account. For example, if a stock is sold in a taxable account and repurchased in a tax-deferred account, wash sale rules will apply.

DIVIDEND DATES

- Declaration date: The date a company's board of directors declares that a dividend will be paid
- Ex-dividend date: The date the market price of a stock adjusts for the dividend. The ex-dividend date is the second business day before the date of record.
- Date of record: The date the company determines who owns stock and is entitled to receive a dividend
- Date of payment: The date the company pays dividends to shareholders

PREFERRED STOCK

PREFERRED STOCK DIVIDENDS

PREFERRED STOCK

- Hybrid security that combines features of both debt and equity
- The price of preferred shares tends to increase as market interest rates decrease
- In the event of corporate bankruptcy, preferred stockholders receive funds before common stockholders
- Preferred shares do not carry voting rights

PREFERRED STOCK DIVIDENDS

- Dividends received on preferred stock are taxed as ordinary income
- Preferred stock dividends must be paid before dividends can be paid to common stockholders
- If a corporation is required to pay unpaid dividends from prior years before paying current dividends to common stockholders, the stock is referred to as cumulative preferred stock

AMERICAN DEPOSITORY RECEIPT (ADR)

EXCHANGE-TRADED FUND (ETF)

AMERICAN DEPOSITORY RECEIPT (ADR)

- Receipt that represents ownership of a foreign stock denominated in US dollars
- Shares of foreign stock are held on deposit at a bank in the company's home country. The foreign bank then issues an ADR, which represents ownership of the underlying stock.
- ADRs may be bought or sold throughout the trading day like stocks
- Dividends are declared in local currencies and paid in US dollars
- ADRs do not eliminate currency risk

EXCHANGE-TRADED FUND (ETF)

- Collection of investments such as stocks, bonds, commodities, or real estate
- ETFs may be bought or sold throughout the trading day like stocks
- Provides diversification
- Minimal transaction costs
- Low turnover
- Tax efficient
- Low fees and expenses

MUTUAL FUND

OPEN-END MUTUAL FUND

MUTUAL FUND

- Collection of investments such as stocks, bonds, commodities, or real estate
- Each investor owns a portion of the mutual fund in relation to the amount of his or her investment
- Provides professional management
- Provides diversification
- Minimal transaction costs
- Two types of mutual funds are open-end and closed-end funds

---

OPEN-END MUTUAL FUND

- A mutual fund that issues new shares when investors buy existing shares
- There is no limit to the number of shares an open-end mutual fund may issue
- Purchase price is based on the fund's net asset value (NAV)
- The majority of mutual funds are open-end funds

CLOSED-END MUTUAL FUND

_____

NET ASSET VALUE (NAV)

CLOSED-END MUTUAL FUND

- A mutual fund with a fixed number of shares that trade on the secondary market after original issue
- Closed-end mutual funds have a fixed capital structure
- Purchase price is based on supply and demand
- Shares may sell at a premium or discount to their net asset value
- Shares are not redeemed directly by the mutual fund

NET ASSET VALUE (NAV)

- The price an investor pays to purchase shares of an open-end mutual fund
- NAV = (total value of investment − liabilities) / shares outstanding
- NAV is calculated once at the end of the trading day

TURNOVER RATE

INTERNATIONAL &
GLOBAL MUTUAL FUNDS

TURNOVER RATE

- Turnover rate = gross proceeds from sale of securities / total NAV
- Measures the level of a mutual fund's trading activity
- A mutual fund with a high turnover rate will require more active management and will charger higher expenses
- The higher the turnover rate, the less tax efficient the mutual fund will be
- A mutual fund with a high turnover rate is best positioned in a tax-deferred account

---

INTERNATIONAL & GLOBAL MUTUAL FUNDS

- International mutual funds may invest in securities from all countries except the investor's home country
- Global mutual funds may invest in securities both inside and outside the investor's home country

HEDGE FUND

UNIT INVESTMENT TRUST (UIT)

HEDGE FUND

- Privately offered fund of securities to accredited investors
- Provides a flexible investment strategy including long, short, leverage, and derivative trading
- High minimum investment requirement
- Investment manager is paid a performance fee

UNIT INVESTMENT TRUST (UIT)

- Registered investment company that buys and holds a fixed portfolio of stocks, bonds, or other securities
- Units are sold to investors for a typical cost of $1,000
- Units may be bought or sold on the secondary market
- Upon termination of a UIT, any remaining securities in the trust will be sold and proceeds will be paid to investors
- Low fees and expenses

GUARANTEED INVESTMENT CONTRACT (GIC)

REAL ESTATE

GUARANTEED INVESTMENT CONTRACT (GIC)

- Contract issued by an insurance company that guarantees repayment of principal and interest for a specific period of time
- Provides a guaranteed, low rate of return
- Has a maturity of five years or less
- Commonly offered as an investment option in 401(k) plans
- GICs are sold primarily to pension plans

REAL ESTATE

- Provides a long-term hedge against inflation
- Offers tax-shelter potential
- Lacks liquidity
- Real estate categories:
  - Commercial
  - Industrial
  - Land
  - Residential

REAL ESTATE
INVESTMENT TRUST (REIT)

TYPES OF REITs

REAL ESTATE INVESTMENT TRUST (REIT)

- Professionally managed investment company that invests in a diversified portfolio of real estate properties and mortgages
- May be publicly or privately held
- REITs are required to distribute 90% of taxable income to shareholders in the form of dividends
- REIT shareholders are not subject to double taxation
- Losses from a REIT cannot be passed through to investors to deduct personally

---

TYPES OF REITs

- Equity REIT
- Mortgage REIT
- Hybrid REIT

EQUITY REIT

MORTGAGE REIT

EQUITY REIT

- Participates in the acquisition, management, renovation, and sale of real estate
- Takes ownership positions in commercial, industrial, and residential properties
- Generates income through capital gains and rental income
- Provides a long-term hedge against inflation

MORTGAGE REIT

- Loans money for mortgages to real estate owners
- Purchases existing mortgages
- Purchases mortgage-backed securities
- Generates income through interest earned on mortgage loans
- Provides a high level of current income

HYBRID REIT

REAL ESTATE MORTGAGE
INVESTMENT CONDUIT (REMIC)

HYBRID REIT

- Combines features of both equity REITs and mortgage REITs
- Generates income through capital gains and rental income similar to equity REITs
- Generates income through interest earned on mortgage loans similar to mortgage REITs

---

REAL ESTATE MORTGAGE INVESTMENT CONDUIT (REMIC)

- Self-liquidating entity that invests in real estate mortgages and mortgage-backed securities
- Combines the predictable cash flow of a bond with the high yield of a mortgage-backed security
- Investors receive a specified cash flow from the underlying mortgages
- REMICs have a limited life that terminates when the underlying mortgages are repaid

ASSET-BACKED SECURITY

MORTGAGE-BACKED SECURITY

ASSET-BACKED SECURITY

- Financial security backed by a loan, lease, receivable, or other debt
- May be offered through an expedited SEC registration process known as a "shelf offering", or through a private placement that is exempt from SEC registration

---

MORTGAGE-BACKED SECURITY

- Financial security that represents a claim on the cash flows from a pool of mortgage loans, most commonly on residential property
- Mortgage loans are purchased from banks, mortgage companies, and other issuers and then collected into pools by a government or private entity. The entity then issues securities that represent claims on the principal and interest payments made by borrowers on the loans in the pool.
- Mortgage-backed securities are issued by Ginnie Mae, Fannie Mae, and Freddie Mac

CALL OPTION

LONG & SHORT CALL OPTIONS

CALL OPTION

- An option to buy a specific number of shares of stock during a specific period at a predetermined price
- Buyer of a call option expects the price of the underlying stock to increase
- Seller (writer) of a call option expects the price of the underlying stock to decrease. An investor sells a call option when seeking premium income.
- An investor who expects a large increase in a stock's price should buy a call option
- An investor who expects a small decrease in a stock's price should sell a call option
- Standard expiration period for a call option is nine months

---

LONG & SHORT CALL OPTIONS

- Long call option
  - Maximum gain is unlimited
  - Maximum loss is limited to the premium paid
- Short call option
  - Maximum gain is limited to the premium received
  - Maximum loss is unlimited

PUT OPTION

LONG & SHORT PUT OPTIONS

PUT OPTION

- An option to sell a specific number of shares of stock during a specific period at a predetermined price
- Buyer of a put option expects the price of the underlying stock to decrease
- Seller (writer) of a put option expects the price of the underlying stock to increase. An investor sells a put option when seeking premium income.
- An investor who expects a large decrease in a stock's price should buy a put option
- An investor who expects a small increase in a stock's price should sell a put option
- Standard expiration period for a put option is nine months

LONG & SHORT PUT OPTIONS

- Long put option
  - Maximum gain is limited to the strike price minus the premium paid
  - Maximum loss is limited to the premium paid
- Short put option
  - Maximum gain is limited to the premium received
  - Maximum loss is limited to the strike price minus the premium received

OPTION HEDGING STRATEGIES

BLACK-SCHOLES OPTION PRICING MODEL

OPTION HEDGING STRATEGIES

- <u>Collar</u>: Simultaneously purchasing a protective put and selling a covered call
- <u>Covered call</u>: Selling a call option while holding shares of the underlying stock
- <u>Protective put</u>: Purchasing a put option while holding shares of the underlying stock
- <u>Spread</u>: Simultaneously purchasing and selling an option on the same side or position within the market
- <u>Straddle</u>: Simultaneously purchasing a call option and a put option on the same stock at the same time

----

BLACK-SCHOLES OPTION PRICING MODEL

- Model used to determine the price of a call option of a non-dividend paying stock
- Assumes call options are European style (exercisable only at the expiration date) and not American style (exercisable any time before the expiration date)
- Factors used in the model include the stock price, strike price, volatility, time to expiration, and the risk-free rate

LONG-TERM EQUITY ANTICIPATION SECURITY (LEAP)

————————————

STOCK RIGHT

LONG-TERM EQUITY ANTICIPATION SECURITY (LEAP)

- Publicly traded option
- Has an expiration greater than one year
- The premium to purchase a LEAP is greater than the premium to purchase a standard option because of the longer time to expiration

––––––––––––––––

STOCK RIGHT

- The holder of a stock right is permitted to buy shares of a company's common stock at a predetermined price that is below market value
- One right is issued for each share of common stock held by an investor. This allows the issuing company to raise money in a manner that favors existing shareholders.
- Stock rights expire within a few weeks after issue

WARRANT

———————————

FUTURES CONTRACT

WARRANT

- The holder of a warrant has the option to purchase securities from the issuer at a predetermined price within a specific time period
- Warrants have a longer term to expiration than stock rights and may not expire for several years
- Warrants may be attached to new debt or preferred issues to act as "sweeteners", making them more attractive to buyers

---

FUTURES CONTRACT

- An agreement to buy or sell a specific quantity of a commodity or financial currency at a predetermined price on a specific future date
- Commodities include bulk goods, such as grains, metals, and foods
- The holder of a futures contract may purchase an offsetting contract that cancels the original position, rather than receiving delivery of the commodity
- Futures trading is regulated by the Commodity Futures Trading Commission (CFTC)

TANGIBLE ASSETS

INVESTMENT RISK

TANGIBLE ASSETS

- Lack marketability and liquidity
- Lack government regulation
- Not subject to a strong secondary market
- Tangible assets include collectibles, antiques, artwork, electronics, etc.

INVESTMENT RISK

- The possibility that an investment's actual return will be less than its expected return
- Two types of investment risk are systematic risk and non-systematic risk
- Total investment risk = systematic risk + non-systematic risk

SYSTEMATIC RISK

TYPES OF SYSTEMATIC RISK

SYSTEMATIC RISK

- The risk associated with the entire market
- Systematic risk can only be minimized, but cannot be eliminated through diversification
- Also referred to as non-diversifiable risk

TYPES OF SYSTEMATIC RISK

Types of systematic risk form the acronym "PRIME"
- Purchasing power risk
- Reinvestment risk
- Interest rate risk
- Market risk
- Exchange rate risk

NON-SYSTEMATIC RISK

TYPES OF NON-SYSTEMATIC RISK

NON-SYSTEMATIC RISK

- The risk associated with a particular company, industry, or sector
- Non-systematic risk cay be eliminated through diversification
- Non-systematic risk cay be avoided by not investing in the particular securities that exhibit the risk
- Also referred to as unsystematic risk, diversifiable risk, and specific risk

———————

TYPES OF NON-SYSTEMATIC RISK

- Business risk
- Default risk
- Financial risk
- Management risk
- Political risk
- Regulatory risk
- Tax risk

BUSINESS RISK

FINANCIAL RISK

BUSINESS RISK

- The risk inherent in company operations
- The risk that a company's cash flows will not be sufficient to pay operating expenses

---

FINANCIAL RISK

- The risk associated with a company's decision to use debt as part of its capital structure
- Companies that issue debt have a higher degree of financial risk than companies financed by equity

INVESTMENT FORMULA VARIABLES

INVESTMENT FORMULA VARIABLES

INVESTMENT FORMULA VARIABLES

α = alpha (Jensen's alpha)

β = beta

ΔP = change in bond price

Δy = change in interest rates

R^2 = coefficient of determination

CV = coefficient of variation

ρ = correlation coefficient

c = coupon

COV = covariance

D_0 = dividend today

D_1 = dividend one year from today

D = duration

g = growth rate of dividend

_____

INVESTMENT FORMULA VARIABLES

Par = par value of a bond

P = price

r = return

r_m = return of the market

r_p = return of the portfolio

r_f = risk-free rate

S = Sharpe

σ = standard deviation

t = time

T = Treynor

V = value

W = weight

y = yield to maturity

CONSTANT DIVIDEND
GROWTH MODEL

STANDARD DEVIATION

CONSTANT DIVIDEND GROWTH MODEL

- Model that determines the intrinsic value of a stock based on future dividends that grow at a constant rate
- The constant dividend growth model may be expressed as:
  - $V = D_1 / (r - g)$, where $D_1 = D_0 (1 + g)$
  - $r = (D_1 / P) + g$, where $D_1 = D_0 (1 + g)$

_____

STANDARD DEVIATION

- Measures the total amount of risk present in an investor's portfolio
- The standard deviation of an investor's portfolio must be less than or equal to the weighted average of the standard deviation of returns of the individual securities
- Example
  - Calculate the standard deviation for the following set of investment returns: +8%, -7%, +6%, and -2%
  - Keystrokes using the HP 12c calculator:

    8Σ

    $7\ CHS\ \Sigma$

    6Σ

    $2\ CHS\ \Sigma$

    Blue g s = 6.99405

BETA

CAPITAL ASSET
PRICING MODEL (CAPM)

BETA

- Measures the amount of systematic risk present in an investor's portfolio
- The formula to calculate beta may be expressed as:
  - $\beta_i = (COV_{im} / \sigma^2_m)$
  - $\beta_i = [(\rho_{im} \times \sigma_i) / \sigma_m]$
- Portfolio beta can be positive, negative, or equal to zero
- A portfolio with a beta of 1.0 has systematic risk only, and the portfolio will move in tandem with the overall market

---

CAPITAL ASSET PRICING MODEL (CAPM)

- $r_i = r_f + (r_m - r_f) \beta_i$
- Calculates an investor's required rate of return
- CAPM is based on the following assumptions:
  - Investors have the same expectations about the risk-return relationship of assets
  - Investors have the same single-period time horizon
  - Investors can borrow and lend money at the risk-free rate
  - There are no transaction costs, taxes, or inflation

SHARPE RATIO

———————

TREYNOR RATIO

SHARPE RATIO

- $S_p = (r_p - r_f) / \sigma_p$
- Measures the risk-adjusted performance of a non-diversified portfolio

---

TREYNOR RATIO

- $T_p = (r_p - r_f) / B_p$
- Measures the risk-adjusted performance of a diversified portfolio

JENSEN'S ALPHA

CORRELATION COEFFICIENT

JENSEN'S ALPHA

- $\alpha_p = r_p - [r_f + (r_m - r_f)\, \beta_p]$
- An absolute measure of the investment performance of a diversified portfolio

---

CORRELATION COEFFICIENT

- $\rho_{ij} = COV_{ij} / (\sigma_i \times \sigma_j)$
- Measures the interdependence of investment returns for two securities
- The correlation coefficient is expressed as a value between -1 and +1
- −1: Two securities are perfectly negatively correlated and their investment returns move opposite each other
- 0: There is no correlation between the investment returns of two securities. They move independently.
- +1: Two securities are perfectly positively correlated and their investment returns move together in the same direction

COEFFICIENT OF DETERMINATION

COEFFICIENT OF VARIATION

COEFFICIENT OF DETERMINATION

- The coefficient of determination (R^2) measures systematic risk
- $1 - R^2$ = unsystematic risk
- R^2 is expressed as a value between 0 and 1
- If R^2 is high (>0.60), then beta is the relevant measure to use when comparing securities. The beta measures are Jensen's alpha and Treynor.
- If R^2 is low (<0.60), then standard deviation is the relevant measure to use when comparing securities. The standard deviation measure is Sharpe.

COEFFICIENT OF VARIATION

- Measures how widely dispersed investment returns are from the mean
- A risk-averse investor prefers a low coefficient of variation
- CV = standard deviation / expected return
- Example:
  - Security A has an expected return of 7% and a standard deviation of 10%. Security B has an expected return of 5% and a standard deviation of 8%. Which security would a risk-averse investor prefer based on the coefficient of variation?
  - CV of Security A = 0.10 / 0.07 = 1.43
    CV of Security B = 0.08 / 0.05 = 1.60
  - A risk-averse investor would prefer Security A

COVARIANCE

SKEWNESS

COVARIANCE

- Measures the degree to which the returns of two securities move together
- Positive covariance indicates the returns of two securities tend to move together in the same direction
- Negative covariance indicates the returns of two securities tend to move opposite each other
- $COV = (\rho) \times (\sigma_1) \times (\sigma_2)$
- Example:
  - Assume that Security A has a standard deviation of 5.5% and Security B has a standard deviation of 8.0%. The correlation coefficient between the two securities is +0.30. What is the covariance of the two securities?
  - $COV = (0.30) \times (5.5) \times (8.0) = 13.2$

SKEWNESS

- Measures the deviation between the actual returns of a probability distribution and the arithmetic mean
- Positively skewed distribution
  - Tail on the right side of a probability distribution is longer than the tail on the left side
  - The mean is greater than the median, which is greater than the mode
- Negatively skewed distribution
  - Tail on the left side of a probability distribution is longer than the tail on the right side
  - The mean is less than the median, which is less than the mode

KURTOSIS

_____

GEOMETRIC MEAN

KURTOSIS

- Measures the tail thickness of a probability distribution
- A fat tail (high kurtosis) indicates investment returns are widely dispersed from the mean, and therefore exhibit more total risk
- A thin tail (low kurtosis) indicates investment returns are bunched towards the mean, and therefore exhibit less total risk
- A risk-averse investor prefers low kurtosis

GEOMETRIC MEAN

- Geometric Mean = $[(X_1) \times (X_2) \times (X_3)........(X_n)]^{1/n} - 1$
- Example:
  - Calculate the geometric mean for the following set of investment returns: +15%, -7%, +8%
  - GM = $[(1.15) \times (0.93) \times (1.08)]^{1/3} - 1$
    GM = 4.92%

HOLDING PERIOD RETURN

REAL & NOMINAL RETURN

HOLDING PERIOD RETURN

- HPR = [(sale price – purchase price) + dividend] / purchase price
- Example:
  - What is the holding period return for an investment that was purchased for $82, paid a $4 dividend, and was later sold for $100?
  - HPR = [($100 - $82) + $4] / $82 = 26.83%
- If an investment's holding period is greater than one year, the holding period return overstates the true return on an annual basis
- If an investment's holding period is less than one year, the holding period return understates the true return on an annual basis

---

REAL & NOMINAL RETURN

- Real return = nominal return - inflation
- Real return is an investment's rate of return after adjusting for inflation
- Nominal return is an investment's rate of return without adjusting for inflation

INTERNAL RATE OF RETURN (IRR)

RULE OF 72

INTERNAL RATE OF RETURN (IRR)

- The rate of return that causes the net present value of all cash flows received from an investment to equal zero
- IRR is used to compare the profitability of investments
- Example:
  - What is the IRR of a 1-year investment in a REIT, if $100 is invested at the beginning of each month and the end of year value is $1,300?
  - Begin Mode
    FV = $1,300
    n = 1 x 12 = 12
    PMT = -$100
    PV = 0
    IRR = ? = 1.2253 x 12 = 14.70

RULE OF 72

- Method used to determine the length of time it takes for an investment to double in value
- Assumes a fixed annual rate of interest
- Example:
  - If an investment earns a 6% annual return, how many years will it take for the investment to double in value?
  - 72 / 6 = 12 years

TAXABLE EQUIVALENT YIELD

_____

PERCENTAGE CHANGE
IN BOND PRICE

TAXABLE EQUIVALENT YIELD

- Taxable equivalent yield = tax free yield / (1 – marginal tax rate)
- Example:
  - What is the taxable equivalent yield of a municipal bond that has a tax free yield of 6%? Assume the investor is in the 28% tax bracket.
  - TEY = 0.06 / (1 – 0.28)
    TEY = 8.33%

PERCENTAGE CHANGE
IN BOND PRICE

The percentage change in bond price is determined by:

- $[\Delta P / P] = -D [\Delta y / (1 + y)]$

LIQUIDITY RATIOS

ACTIVITY RATIOS

LIQUIDITY RATIOS

- Cash ratio = (cash + marketable securities) / current liabilities
- Current ratio = current assets / current liabilities
- Quick ratio = (current assets – inventory) / current liabilities

---

ACTIVITY RATIOS

- Average collection period = annual receivables / sales per day
- Fixed asset turnover ratio = annual sales / fixed assets
- Inventory turnover ratio = annual sales / average inventory level

PROFITABILITY RATIOS

MODERN PORTFOLIO THEORY

PROFITABILITY RATIOS

- Net profit margin = net income / annual sales
- Operating profit margin = earnings before interest and taxes / annual sales
- Return on assets = net income / total assets
- Return on equity = net income / shareholders' equity

MODERN PORTFOLIO THEORY

- Theory introduced by Harry Markowitz that identifies an investor's optimal portfolio as being located at the point of tangency between the investor's indifference curve and the efficient frontier of available investments
- MPT is based on the following assumptions:
  - For a given level of risk, investors prefer higher returns to lower returns
  - Investors are rational and naturally risk-averse
  - Increased risk is an inherent part of achieving higher returns

MARKOWITZ
EFFICIENT FRONTIER

CAPITAL MARKET LINE

MARKOWITZ EFFICIENT FRONTIER

- The efficient frontier is the set of optimal portfolios for any given investor as defined by Modern Portfolio Theory
- Changing the proportion of securities already invested in a portfolio will move an investor's position along the efficient frontier, but will not shift it
- Selecting securities with lower coefficients of correlation between them will reduce risk and shift the efficient frontier upward and to the left

---

CAPITAL MARKET LINE

- $r_p = r_f + \sigma_p \left[(r_m - r_f) / \sigma_m \right]$
- The capital market line is the tangent line to the efficient frontier that passes through the risk-free rate on the expected return axis. The point of tangency corresponds to a portfolio on the efficient frontier
- All portfolios located along the capital market line are efficient portfolios

SECURITY MARKET LINE

EFFICIENT MARKET HYPOTHESIS

SECURITY MARKET LINE

- $r_i = r_f + (r_m - r_f)\, B_i$
- The security market line determines if a security being considered for inclusion in an investor's portfolio offers an adequate expected return for the level of risk assumed
- The security market line is the graphical representation of CAPM

EFFICIENT MARKET HYPOTHESIS

- Theory that suggests investors are unable to outperform the market on a consistent basis
- According to EMH, the market efficiently prices securities so that investors cannot buy undervalued stocks or sell overvalued stocks on a consistent basis
- Excess investment returns are only temporary and will regress to the mean
- Daily fluctuations in stock prices are a result of a random walk pattern

EFFICIENT MARKET HYPOTHESIS FORMS

EFFICIENT MARKET HYPOTHESIS: WEAK FORM

EFFICIENT MARKET HYPOTHESIS FORMS

- Weak form
- Semi-strong form
- Strong form

EFFICIENT MARKET HYPOTHESIS: WEAK FORM

- All security information, including historical prices and volume data, is fully reflected in stock prices
- Technical analysis will not produce returns in excess of the market
- Fundamental analysis may produce returns in excess of the market
- Insider information may produce returns in excess of the market

EFFICIENT MARKET HYPOTHESIS: SEMI-STRONG FORM

EFFICIENT MARKET HYPOTHESIS: STRONG FORM

EFFICIENT MARKET HYPOTHESIS: SEMI-STRONG FORM

- All public information is fully reflected in stock prices
- Technical analysis will not produce returns in excess of the market
- Fundamental analysis will not produce returns in excess of the market
- Insider information may produce returns in excess of the market

---

EFFICIENT MARKET HYPOTHESIS: STRONG FORM

- All public and private information is fully reflected in stock prices
- All information is cost-free and available to all investors simultaneously
- Technical analysis will not produce returns in excess of the market
- Fundamental analysis will not produce returns in excess of the market
- Insider information will not produce returns in excess of the market

TOP-DOWN ANALYSIS

BOTTOM-UP ANALYSIS

TOP-DOWN ANALYSIS

Method of investment analysis that involves the following process:

- Step 1: Examine the global economy
- Step 2: Examine a specific economy
- Step 3: Examine a specific industry
- Step 4: Examine a specific company

BOTTOM-UP ANALYSIS

Method of investment analysis that involves the following process:

- Step 1: Examine a specific company
- Step 2: Examine a specific industry
- Step 3: Examine a specific economy
- Step 4: Examine the global economy

TECHNICAL ANALYSIS

BEHAVIORAL FINANCE

TECHNICAL ANALYSIS

- <u>Moving average</u>: Graphical representation of a security's average price over a period of time
- <u>Trendline</u>: Line that indicates the direction and speed that a security's price moves over a period of time
- <u>Support and resistance levels</u>: Support is the level at which demand is strong enough to prevent security prices from declining further. Resistance is the level at which selling activity is strong enough to prevent security prices from rising further.

BEHAVIORAL FINANCE

- Confirmation bias
  - An investor's tendency to value information that supports his or her previously established decision, even if that decision was unwise
  - May explain why investors are slow to sell underperforming stocks
- Prospect theory
  - Investors fear losses more than they value gains
  - Investors will often choose the smaller of two potential gains if it avoids a highly probable loss

STOCK MARKET ANOMALIES

_____

MARGIN CALL

STOCK MARKET ANOMALIES

- <u>January effect</u>: Stock prices tend to increase in the month of January
- <u>Neglected firm effect</u>: Lesser-known companies tend to outperform better-known companies. "Neglected" means few analysts follow the stock.
- <u>P/E effect</u>: Stocks with low price-earnings ratios tend to outperform stocks with high price-earnings ratios
- <u>Small-firm effect</u>: Small cap stocks tend to outperform large cap stocks
- <u>Value Line anomaly</u>: Stocks rated 1 out of 5 by *Value Line Investment Survey* tend to outperform the overall market

---

MARGIN CALL

- Margin call = stock purchase price x [(1 – initial margin %) / (1 – maintenance margin %)]

INITIAL MARGIN

_____

MAINTENANCE MARGIN

INITIAL MARGIN

- Percentage of a security's purchase price that an investor must pay with cash
- Minimum initial margin is 50% as established by Regulation T of the Federal Reserve Board

---

MAINTENANCE MARGIN

- After a stock is purchased on margin, an investor is required to keep a minimum amount of equity in his or her margin account. This is known as the maintenance margin.
- Minimum maintenance margin is 25% as established by Regulation T of the Federal Reserve Board

ARBITRAGE

_____

ARBITRAGE PRICING THEORY (APT)

ARBITRAGE

- Simultaneously purchasing a security in one market at a lower price, and selling the security in another market at a higher price
- Allows an investor to profit from the distortion in a security's price without taking risk
- Exists as a result of market inefficiencies

————————————

ARBITRAGE PRICING THEORY (APT)

- Calculates the true value and expected return of a security in the absence of arbitrage conditions
- According to APT, a security's price in different markets will not differ for a significant length of time because the unexpected change that caused the arbitrage opportunity will be eliminated at an equilibrium point in the future

FACTORS AFFECTING
ARBITRAGE PRICING THEORY

SECURITIES LEGISLATION

FACTORS AFFECTING ARBITRAGE PRICING THEORY

Arbitrage pricing theory is affected by unexpected changes in:
- Gross national product
- Inflation
- Interest rates
- Investor confidence
- Risk premiums

SECURITIES LEGISLATION

- Securities Act of 1933
- Securities Exchange Act of 1934
- Investment Company Act of 1940
- Securities Investor Protection Act of 1970

SECURITIES ACT OF 1933

SECURITIES EXCHANGE
ACT OF 1934

SECURITIES ACT OF 1933

- Regulates new issues of securities
- Requires that investors receive specific financial information regarding securities being offered for public sale
- Prohibits deceit, misrepresentation, and fraud in the sale of securities
- Enables investors to make informed decisions regarding securities

---

SECURITIES EXCHANGE ACT OF 1934

- Regulates secondary trading of securities
- Regulates corporate reporting, proxy solicitations, and tender offers
- Created the Securities and Exchange Commission (SEC) and gave it broad authority over all aspects of the securities industry
- SEC has the power to register, regulate, and oversee brokerage firms

INVESTMENT COMPANY
ACT OF 1940

SECURITIES INVESTOR
PROTECTION ACT OF 1970

INVESTMENT COMPANY ACT OF 1940

- Regulates mutual funds
- Intended to minimize conflicts of interest that arise during investment company operations
- Requires investment companies to disclose their financial status and investment policies to investors on a regular basis
- Does not allow the SEC to directly supervise the investment decisions made by mutual fund companies or judge the merits of their investments

---

SECURITIES INVESTOR PROTECTION ACT OF 1970

- Regulates brokerage firms
- Created the Securities Investor Protection Corporation (SIPC) to protect investors against brokerage firm bankruptcies
- If a brokerage firm becomes insolvent, each investor is protected up to $500,000, including a maximum of $250,000 for cash claims

ABOUT THE AUTHOR

Matthew Brandeburg is a Certified Financial Planner in Columbus, Ohio. He serves as the Chief Operating Officer for a fee-only financial planning firm with over $500 million in assets under management and he's an active member of the National Association of Personal Financial Advisors (NAPFA). Matthew is the author of the books "Financial Planning For Your First Job," "Your Guide to the CFP Certification Exam," and "CFP Certification Exam Practice Question Workbook." In addition, he teaches the class "Financial Planning in your 20s and 30s" at Ohio State University.

INDEX

Made in the USA
San Bernardino, CA
24 November 2017